Options Trading

Easiest Beginners Simplified Guide, Effective Profitable Strategies - Learn the Foundamental Basics of Options Trading and Start Today

Tony Toson

© Copyright 2019 by Tony Toson

All rights reserved.

This Book is provided with the sole purpose of providing relevant information on a specific topic for which every reasonable effort has been made to ensure that it is both accurate and reasonable. Nevertheless, by purchasing this Book you consent to the fact that the author, as well as the publisher, are in no way experts on the topics contained herein, regardless of any claims as such that may be made within. As such, any suggestions or recommendations that are made within are done so purely for entertainment value. It is recommended that you always consult a professional prior to undertaking any of the advice or techniques discussed within.

This is a legally binding declaration that is considered both valid and fair by both the Committee of Publishers Association and the American Bar Association and should be considered as legally binding within the United States.

The reproduction, transmission, and duplication of any of the content found herein, including any specific or extended information will be done as an illegal act regardless of the end form the information ultimately takes. This includes copied versions of the work both physical, digital and audio unless express consent of the Publisher is provided beforehand. Any additional rights reserved.

Furthermore, the information that can be found within the pages described forthwith shall be considered both accurate and truthful when it comes to freely available information and general consent. As such, any use, correct or incorrect, of the provided information will render the Publisher free of responsibility as to the actions taken outside of their direct purview. Regardless, there are zero scenarios where the original author or the Publisher can be deemed liable in any fashion for any damages or hardships that may result from any of the information discussed within.

Finally, any of the content found within is ultimately intended for entertainment purposes and should be thought of and acted on as such. Due to its inherently ephemeral nature, nothing discussed within should be taken as an assurance of quality, even when the words and deeds described herein indicated otherwise. Trademarks and copyrights mentioned within are done for informational purposes in line with fair use and should not be seen as an endorsement from the copyright or trademark holder.

Table of Contents

Introduction 6
Chapter 1: Options Trading Basics 8
Chapter 2: Build Your Personal Trading Plan 28
Chapter 3: Fundamental Analysis 47
Chapter 4: Technical Analysis 60
Chapter 5: Strategies for Beginners 78
Chapter 6: Options Trading in the Forex Market 93
Chapter 7: Tips for Success 106
Chapter 8: Mistakes to Avoid 119
Conclusion 130

Introduction

Options trading offers numerous benefits to several different types of investors that make it superior to more traditional forms of investing, once you get the hang of it.

It is not without its own unique quirks that can leave you broke if not handled with care, however, which is why the following chapters will discuss everything that you need to know in order to ensure that you can benefit from everything that options trading has to offer. For starters, you will learn about the various types of options and how to utilize each properly along with the ideal mindset for doing so and the proper to terminology to go along with it. From there, you will learn about the various types of risk and how being aware of them can save you from making a huge mistake. Once you understand the risk, you will be ready to learn about all of the various factors that can influence the price of a specific option during its lifetime.

With that taken care of, you will be ready to make your first trade, including creating a personalized trading plan and a step by step walkthrough of what you will need to do in order to successfully place a trade. From there you will learn several important strategies that all options trading beginners should know in order to maximize your trading success. Next up you will learn how to interpret all of the data you will have been collecting on all of your trades up until this point and how it can make you a more successful trader all-around. Finally, you will learn a number of important tips for success that should help push your successful trade percentage over the top.

With so many choices out there when it comes to consuming this type of content, it is appreciated that you've chosen this one. Plenty of care and effort went into ensuring it contains as many interesting and useful tidbits as possible, please enjoy!

Chapter 1: Options Trading Basics

What Are Options?

It's the most basic of questions, and one that even truly experienced options traders often have to think about before they can provide an answer. This is not for lack of experience on their part, but because the mechanics and utility of options can be complicated. Their function in the market is one of upmost importance, but how they are used to hedge bets and lower the exposure of risk for investors is still complicated. An option is a contract that allows a trader to buy or sell a stock for a certain price that is different from the current trading price, all at a later date. This is the exact definition of an option, and indeed in a single sentence it is a lot of information to take in, so let's use some examples to help guide us, starting with a real world

scenario outside of the stock market for why you would possibly want to use an option.

Let's suppose that you are interested in buying a car on Craigslist or eBay. The car is a model and brand that you are very interested in. The seller of the car is asking for $8000 and they are located in a city 200 miles from your home. You are interested in the car, enough so that you would be very disappointed to go to that location and find out that it has already been sold. You work during the week however and a 200 mile road trip is out of the question. To incentivize the seller of the car to hold onto it until you arrive, you offer $150 for the right to buy the car this coming weekend. For the seller, they gain $150 in the immediate and only have to hold onto the car for a few days. For you, you lose $150 but now have the car reserved to buy it.

This is a basic form of the option contract, albeit the underlying asset it quite different. Continuing with this example, you travel the distance to meet the seller and inspect the car. You find that it is in terrible condition, a shape far worse than the online photos showed. You decide that it is not worth the $8000 and walk away from the deal entirely. Even though you paid the $150 to reserve the right to buy the car, you did not have to exercise this option once the weekend came and you actually saw what the car was worth. This is how options got their namesake, as the contract reserves the right for you to buy the car but does not mean that you are forced to buy the car.

It is clear what you gained from this contract and the expenses that you incurred, but what about the seller of the car? They gained $150 in the immediate, and they will keep this money even though you didn't buy the product. They lost the right to sell the car in the intervening time between your $150 contract and the time in which you actually saw the car; they could have received multiple offers on the car but would have had to turn them down – the car was reserved for you.

We can see the advantages and disadvantages for both the buyer and the seller of the option contract – the buyer has gained the right to buy the car at a pre-agreed upon price at a later date but loses $150 in the immediate. The seller gains $150 but loses the right to sell the car before you arrive over the weekend. This is a model option based on a different underlying asset but demonstrates many of the key points of how options function in financial markets; contracts between two parties that allow the exchange of goods at a later time if certain conditions are met. In markets, the condition that is met for an option to be used is the trading price of an option (a more detailed example will come in chapter 2), and in this example, that is represented by the buyer inspecting the car when they actually meet the seller.

An option has specific parameters that need to be known by both parties for a contract to be bought or sold. These parameters come in four major measures, and they exist even in the example above with the car, albeit they are slightly abstracted. These parameters are the contract price, the contract expiration, the strike price, and the exercise price. In the example above with our car, we had the contract price ($150), the contract expiration (the weekend when the buyer meets the seller), the strike price ($8000), and the exercise price (the buyer inspecting the car and determining if they want it).

These four parameters are sold in two primary forms of options, calls, and puts. In their most basic forms, a call option is one where the buyer expects the price of a commodity to rise, whereas a put option is one where the buyer of the option expects the price of a commodity to fall. These are labeled as calls and puts so that traders can gain the information needed about an option, as well as the intent of the buyer or seller, very quickly by merely glancing at the information.

If you are new to the world of trading, this is quite a bit of information to take in, but with an example of each in the coming chapters, you should be able to internalize the difference between these two options and know their usage. For now, keep in mind that the example with the car is not fundamentally different from how an option works; merely the underlying asset is different.

Getting Started

Brokers: As a starting trader, your broker will be very important to you. Not just because you will want one with the lowest cost per trade, but also because you want the best research tools available to you. I highly recommend that you start with EOption Review – this brokerage house has the lowest transaction cost per option bought or sold, and will be extremely useful when making the most profit off of trading a small number of options. Later in this chapter, you will see that the amount that you invest in an option is a function of your total investment fund. Assuming that since you are at the beginner level and your total investment fund is not all that large, the brokerage fees can add up quite quickly, and so this is a great firm for starting off with small trades.

For the best research tools available, you will want to go with Charles Schwab Review. This is a broker that you might never even want to trade through, but rather make an account, keep some money there, and use their tools for finding the most up to date prices/indexes for different options. Their tools feature a number of neat applications, like predictions on what the cost of options will be a few months down the line based on assumptions that a trader inputs. This is not an account that you need to create right away, but is one that will almost certainly be useful to you in the future as you continue to trade.

Aside from these two brokerage houses, you will have lots of different choices for picking a broker. I recommend just dealing with these two to start, and even from these, you will probably want to avoid Charles Schwab as you find your way and make a few trades first. Other brokerage firms offer tool sets that are not as good as Schwab or offer a transaction fee per trade that will be more expensive than EOption.

Bid Price/Ask Price: In our basic examples that covered the simple strategies of calls and puts, we were working with some very basic rules. For the sake of simplicity and to explain the mechanics of options, I removed the cost per transaction for options. This means more than just removing the fees that a broker would collect, but also not having to worry about a key aspect of the options market – the bid price and ask price for options. You will be relying on a lot of different sources to decide what commodities to write or buy options for, and chief among them will be the different exchanges that sell options.

These are indexes that list the most frequently purchased options, giving lots of information about the volume of options being sold, how they are being written, and when most of them are expected to expire. The most key piece of information will be the bid and ask price for options. The ask price is what option sellers are trying to get for selling one contract. The bid price is what buyers are willing to pay for an option. We refer to the split between them as the spread of the option. This concept may sound complicated, but the premise is actually quite easy when taken with an example.

Suppose that you were interested in purchasing a call option from McDonald's. Don't worry about the strike price, expiration date, or exercise price. All you need to know is that you want to buy a call and that you know the underlying commodity is McDonald's stock. You would refer to an index on your broker's website, or refer to an index from one of the major listing boards, such as the Chicago Board Options Exchange. Here you would find a listing of bid prices, asking prices, and the spread between them. These are typically listed in a per share metric, such that if you wanted to buy one option contract, you would typically be multiplying the ask or bid price by one hundred to get the real cost of the option. This is because options are sold and bought measuring against 100 shares for each options contract. In this case, with the McDonald's stock, the bid price is $4.90 and the ask price is $5.12. The spread, in this case, is then $0.22.

What this means is that a buyer is willing to buy an option on McDonald's stock for $4.90 per share, while a seller is willing to sell an option for $5.12 per share. You will also get a listing of the volume of the number of contracts sold in the last time interval (ranges depending on how you sort the options). The spread is useful because it tells you how much you would immediately lose per share if you bought an option on McDonald's and immediately turned around and sold it. In this case, you would be buying an option for $0.22 more than you would be selling the option, netting you the loss of that spread per share on buying the McDonald's option.

There is a lot of useful information to be gleamed from the bid/ask price, as well as the spread for options contracts. First, it tells an options trader how the supply and demand of a particular option contract matches each other, so that if the spread is quite large, there is either more demand for an option, or it is in limited supply. Two, it tells the options trader how much they could realistically write options for on a particular commodity. Three, and most important to both options traders and general investors, it shows the possible direction of a commodity in the near future.

If the spread is quite large on McDonald's and the volume of calls is quite low, this means that investors believe the stock is due for a reversal in the near future. The lack of options being sold signal that there is a discrepancy in the number of options being offered versus the number of options that actually exist. In simplest terms, you can think of these three metrics, bid, ask and spread, as a way of determining the supply and demand for options on a particular commodity. It will be one of the most useful indexes when determining what commodities to write or buy options for. How you use the information is highly variable on the volume of options sold, whether it is a call or put, and other information about how a company is doing. It is not the end of all tool for determining the direction that a commodity will move, but it is instead just one tool among many.

Searching For Options: The intent of this book is to give a trader all of the information they need to make intelligent trades right away. You are learning about key strategies that are used at every level of trading to make a profit in any type of market. With this intent, I am writing examples that feature the laymen terms for expiration dates, strike prices, etc. How you will actually search for options will be a bit different. For example, say that you want to find calls for Microsoft that expire on March 12, 2018.

This is listed as C-MSFT Mar 18. The first letter refers to whether the option is a call or put, followed by the ticker name of the company, and then the month and two digits of the ending year. To find the specific date, March 12th, you would look through the index of all of the calls that are being sold for Microsoft that expire in March of 2018, and sort by date. This will grant you the ability to find the specific end date that you are looking for.

In searching for options, you will find that indexes list a lot of additional information in addition to the end date, call or put, etc. The lists show metrics for the changes in the overall cost of the option. This is based on the spread of the option overall, with the major metrics showing different ways in which the spread has changed over time. This is highly variable based on where you are looking up an index, but most of the time they will have common information like the percentage change in spread and volume of options for this date being sold.

It is very important that as you are searching for options, you are doing so knowing that there are thousands of options for each company listed every month. Part of the challenge of invoking any of the strategies in this book is a matter of getting good at finding an option that suits your needs. Listing an option to be sold is simple enough, but buying one that will profit you takes some time getting used to. It is for this reason that I highly suggest doing plenty of searching on the brokerage firm of your choice before you start making any purchases. It can be a bit confusing to read listings at first, but a few searches and you'll get the hang of it.

As a final note, nearly all options are listed in the cost of the option per share. For example, a call for Starbucks may be listed as $1.10. The true cost of this option is $110 because the option must be purchased in increments of 100 shares. Also, since you may not be buying the option from the same trader, the call on the second hundred shares is likely to be a different price. It means that looking at the simple value of price per share cannot just be extrapolated to 200 or 1000 shares. You have to figure that the prices are highly flexible, and will not remain the same as you increase the number of calls or puts that you buy of any one company.

Size Of Investment Fund & Amount to invest: The size of your investment fund is going to vary depending on how much you want to put at stake for your options trading future. I make the recommendation that you do not start with an amount of less than $2,000. Any amount more than this is great, but this is really the absolute minimum that you will need to get started. An ideal amount is closer to 4k or 5k. At these sums, your investment in each option can be quite sizeable, with good returns on trades that work well to your favor. It is key that for each trade you make you risk no more than ten percent of your total investment fund.

This is the upper limit of how much you will want to spend on a single option. You should never be spending more than this percentage on a single option because if a trade goes poorly, it limits your ability to spread out risk in the future. Starting at $2,000, this means that each trade you make should be limited to $200. You will find that there are not that many trades that you can conduct with that much money. You will be able to buy a single option, instead of multiples. Also, the brokerage fees will play a more significant role as the percentage that they take from commissions will matter more. Most importantly, it limits the expiration date for your trades.

Keep in mind that it will be, in most cases, a month before you can really determine if a trade has been beneficial to you. This means that you must assume that the trade is in limbo, and cannot count profit until the option is made liquid. In your first month of trading therefore, you can expect to make a maximum of around six trades with a $2,000 investment fund.

This gives you time to learn from your mistakes, learn your style, and figure out how you can improve your trading game.

In regards to determining the amount to invest, remember that writing an option contract will net you some amount of money up front, but that you must calculate what your potential risk is for each contract that you write. As you progress to the next few chapters and start looking at more advanced strategies, you will want to focus on covered calls and puts, as well as plain straddles and strangles. These are strategies that tell you exactly how much money is at risk in each one of your transactions.

If you start writing options for stock that you do not own, the covered aspect of this strategy, you are exposing yourself to a lot of risk for each individual trade. The money that you make in the immediate after writing an option is money that needs to be thought of as still at risk, and not something that you can bank; this is all in addition to knowing what your total exposure to risk for each trade that you make. If calculating your risk based on writing contracts seems difficult right now, that's fine; you will fully understand how to make these calculations when you are done reading the explanations for strategies in the following chapters.

Big Picture Market Utility: Now that you know how calls and puts work, you can start to see the big picture of how options can be used to judge the market. Options are traded on several different markets, such as the Chicago Board Options Exchange (CBOE). These types of exchanges list options on all types of commodities, ranging from stock to futures dealing in oil and crops, such as oranges and coffee. By looking at the price of options, traders that do not even sell or buy options gain a bit of useful information.

They have an additional index to which they can reference to determine if the price of a commodity will rise or fall. Think about it this way: if Apple stock were trading at $120, but thousands of put options were being sold for very high prices on the stock, what does that really say about the confidence in Apple stock? Apple's stock might be trading high, but the thousands of options taken out protecting against the decline of Apple stock, in addition to the high price of these contracts, signals that buyers believe there is a high risk of the exercise price being met, meaning that confidence is actually quite low.

This will lead investors to buy puts on Apple stock, or simply sell the Apple stock that they do own. For others, they might even begin selling call options on Apple stock. You'll remember that a call option is used when a buyer believes that the stock will rise. A seller of call options on Apple stock would be led to believe that if anything the stock is likely to fall, leading them to think that they could sell call options with little chance that the exercise price will ever be met. All of these indexes and exchanges work together to form the big picture of how commodities are really doing, and help predict the direction that they will go in.

What is unique about options trading as it relates to determining market health, is the expiration date associated with these contracts. Contracts don't need to be written for thirty or sixty days; they can be made with expiration dates years from now. This sort of long term bet against or for a commodity tells investors additional information about trader sentiment on particular commodities.

The trading price of similar options with similar expiration dates help form the overall big picture of what the markets will do. The last part of this chapter will discuss the fundamental differences between the European and American options markets – you will likely never trade on European options markets, but keep in mind that there is lots of useful information to be gained by looking at how these options are trading. Getting as much information to price options accordingly is part of the recipe for your success in trading options.

Quick Note About American Versus European Options: In the examples you've seen so far, you saw usage of options as they relate to US financial markets. In Europe the rules regarding options are slightly different, however, the minor differences between them change so much of their function and utility. The difference is that in US markets an option can be used if the exercise price has been met and it is before the expiration date.

In European markets, the option can only be used if the exercise price is met on the date of the expiration.

This may seem like a small difference, but the implications are very far reaching. Note that a trader's ability to buy or sell options contracts is not limited by their home country or where they are trading from, so a European trader has access to US options markets, while US traders have access to European options markets.

The difference in how these options are used in such that the amount of options that flow through US markets far, far exceeds the number that goes through European exchanges. This is because the utility in the US market for options is far wider and can be used in far more conditions, driving the price of options contracts up significantly.

Take for example that you purchase a call option that expires in 30 days. In US markets, the exercise price is met on the twelfth day after the contract was purchased. The buyer of the contract can then use the contract on that day. Suppose that they use the option on the full 100 shares that the option allows, and then on the thirtieth day of the contract the stock price has fallen below the exercise price – it doesn't matter, the buyer has already used the contract. In European markets this functions in the exact opposite manner. A contract buyer has the exercise price met on the twentieth day, but they cannot use the contract. On the expiration date of the contract, the option has fallen below the exercise price that it was trading above just some ten days ago. They cannot use this option because their contract can only be used on the day of the expiration date.

Chapter 2: Build Your Personal Trading Plan

After you have a clear idea of everything that goes into determining the pricing of specific options, you will just about be ready to stop learning theory and start putting it into practice. Before you get started, however, it is important to determine your own personalized trading plan.

Create a plan

The fact of the matter is that there is simply no way you can expect to be successful in the long term when it comes to day trading if you don't have a plan that has been personalized based on your very own strengths and weaknesses. While skipping this section, and finding a generalized trading plan online, may be the fastest way to start trading as soon as possible, it is far from the most efficient.

Determine your current level of skill: In order to ensure that you create a plan with a realistic chance for success, the first thing that you are going to want to do is determine what your current competencies are when it comes to trading in general and the underlying asset you are hoping to focus on specifically. The more experience you have, the more elaborate and ambitious your plan can be but it is important to determine your level of experience honestly as overestimating your experience is only going to make it more difficult for you to start turning a profit in the first place.

During this step, you are also going to want to catalogue your general strengths and weaknesses as they relate to trading in general and options trading specifically. It is especially important to be honest with yourself when it comes to your strengths and weaknesses, especially when it comes to your ability to properly maintain your composure when your emotions are running high. Remember, this isn't a test that you can either pass or fail, it is simply an examination of the ways you can be the most effective trader possible. As such, if you fudge the results then the only person who is going to be losing out is you. With enough forethought, you can maximize your strengths and minimize your weaknesses, leading to overall greater success in both the short and the long term.

Decide how much risk is right for you: When it comes to determining how much risk is the right amount, the final solution is going to be different for each trader. This is because there is no singular amount of risk that is perfect for everyone, the risk is more individualized than that. To get started figuring out the perfect amount of risk for you, the first thing that you will want to do is to determine how much capital you are going to allot solely to trading, as well as what that amount means to you. If you have saved a few thousand dollars in a month or so to give something new a try, then your overall risk is going to be low. If you saved that same amount over nearly a year of dedicated saving then that same amount might represent a much higher risk. Regardless, it is important to never put more into a single trade than you can ever afford to lose.

A good rule of thumb is that each individual trade should encompass no more than 5 percent of your total options trading fund to ensure that a small mistake doesn't end up costing you dearly. What's more, when it comes to deciding to take chances on potential trades you are only going to want to pull the trigger when you have a reasonable suspicion that the trade in question is going to end with you making three times as much in profit as what you originally put in prior to paying any related fees. To determine this amount all you need to do is take the potential payout and divide it by the buy-in amount, if the result is greater than three then you can move ahead with the trade with a clean conscience. This advice is what is known as the risk/reward ratio and it is key to trading in options successfully.

Besides the financial realities of your situation, you are also going to need to consider how much time you ultimately plan on spending concentrating on options trading to the exclusion of all else along with the amount of profit you hope to see in the process. If, after determining the amount of time you hope to spend trading your financial estimates aren't as high as you might like, you can then either change the amount of time you are planning to spend or the amount of risk you are willing to put up with, there are only these three variables to work with. Be wary when it comes to raising your risk too high as major amounts of risk are as likely to lead to major losses as they are too major windfalls.

Prepare yourself: Ideally you will be spending the early hours of the day reading up on the likely state of the market for the moment when it opens so that you can take advantage of your planning as much as possible. As such, when it comes to creating your plan it is important to understand how much time you realistically have to commit to maximizing your trade advantage and what other parts of your life are going to interfere with this preparation. There is certainly money to be made by trading options at less regular hours, but the only way that you will be prepared to do so is if you know about the discrepancy ahead of time and work to minimize its impact as much as possible.

In addition to the daily preparations that will be

required of you, you will also need to be aware of various important due dates, both for your underlying asset of choice as a whole, as well as any holdings you might have specifically. Earnings reports of all types are sure to have a noticeable effect on the market and if you are caught unaware you have no choice but to take a loss that, in many cases, can be quite serious. You will also need to be aware of when any dividend payments are coming due for any options that are related to stocks that you might own. Owning an option does not entitle you to a dividend so you must know when to exercise your options if you hope to maximize your profits at all times.

Understand when you will want to get while the getting is good: When it comes to creating a successful strategy, it is important that you take the time to determine exactly when you are going to want to exit every trade that you make, no matter what. Choosing this point means considering your acceptable level of risk and will ultimately serve to limit your losses, though also doing the same to your profits.

Specifically, this means that when scenarios arise

such as when a stock drops out of the money from a previously profitable position, you will always want to be realistic about the situation and understand that the best thing is to do is sell rather than wait for it come back around, risking even greater losses in the interim. This logic is flawed, and what's worse, will lead to future negative habits if you are lucky enough for it to work out in your favor the first time as it will always result in a loss in the long run.

Instead, you will want to determine what the best strategy is for you and your holdings based on numerous personal factors including other trades you are currently pursuing, what you believe to be an acceptable level of risk and how closely you plan to micromanage each individual trade. Essentially, what this means is that the specific details behind the exit strategy that you choose don't matter, what does matter is that you plan out what it is going to be, before you make your first move, and then stick with it no matter what, even if every emotional cell in your being is telling you to change horses midstream and do something that is almost certainly stupid.

To keep your losses to a minimum, you are going to want to use what is known as stop losses. Stop losses are a way to automatically buy or sell options based on a predetermined set of specifications. As such, they are not terribly useful when it comes to trading in options that are likely to move a great deal in both directions over a short period of time but can be extremely useful in other, more stable, situations. It doesn't matter if you are the holder or the writer, stop losses are a must for everyone involved in the interaction. You will also find that secondary stop orders are also useful when it comes to securing a predetermined amount of profit while still ensuring that you can take advantage of any ongoing positive trends as well. This is done thanks to what is known as a price target which is the amount you feel is realistic to expect to make from the trade in question. You then simply set your first stop loss at this point and then set a second stop loss much higher. This way when the first level of profit is reached you can sell off half of your holdings while still retaining the rest in case the positive trend continues in a big way.

Find the right place to start: Once you know when you are going to get out of any trade that you place, the next thing that you will need to consider is the right time to capitalize on the trend of a specific option. The best way to go about doing this is to consider the amount of risk that you deem acceptable before considering what type of purchase you want to make when you come across an option that meets your criteria for purchase based on your earnings goals and your risk assessment.

As a new options trader, what you are going to likely be the most interested in is making a single option purchase per trade. While this might not seem like a lot, it is important to keep in mind that each option is going to be worth 100 shares which means that it only takes a little bit of movement from the underlying asset to cause significant gains or losses for any trads that you make. This means that you are going to want to be discerning when it comes to choosing the right entry point, one that is relaxed enough to ensure that you aren't waiting days between trades and strict enough that every option you come across doesn't automatically qualify.

Goals

It is important to ultimately consider what goals you

have for trading and how likely each trade is to help move you one step closer to achieving them. A good way to do so is to determine if each of your goals related to options trading is not only realistic but SMART.

The first SMART goal that you set should be one that is at the same time straightforward enough to more or less ensure your success while at the same time being relevant enough to your day to day life that actually succeeding will be a moment that you can easily recall in the future when success on a future goal is not nearly so assured. This way you will start forming the right type of neural pathways as soon as possible, which will then form into patterns which will eventually become habits. With this in mind, you want to start off with a goal that is, at least tangentially connected to the negative pattern that you are the most anxious to start to change. You don't need to have an exact goal in mind at this point, just the start of an idea that you can build into something larger later on. Consider the following to ensure that you are on the right track.

SMART goals are specific: The best goals are the ones that you will always be able to clearly determine where you stand in relation to the goal. The goal should then have a clearly defined fail state as well as state that will clearly let you know when you have crossed the finish line. Specific goals are also going to be much easier to chart out over time as their specificity will lend to clear sub-goals that can be linked to their success or failure.

When you choose a specific goal, you are going to want to guarantee that you have a clear idea of the following details to ensure that you have chosen a goal that is truly specific enough for your needs.

- Who you will need to work with in order to make the goal a reality

- What you will need to do in order to get started on completing the goal

- Where you will need to go in order to see the goal through to completion

- Why you wanted to get started completing the goal in the first place

- When you can realistically expect the goal to be completed

- How you will go about completing the goal in various steps

Measurable: A good goal is one where progress towards success can easily be measured, giving you a feeling of accomplishment and a serotonin boost every time you make another step in the right direction. With your first few goals, it is extremely important to keep them measurable in order to nurture the growth of the proper neural pathways. To determine the metric of success you should be using, start by determining the easiest criteria by which you can measure success.

This metric can either be one that is based on achieving certain predetermined outcomes or one that is based on cold, hard facts, the important thing is that there are clearly defined points that can be used to ensure you are always on the right track. Early goals tend to work better when a success metric is a number that can be easily defined as it helps to be able to constantly see a stream of new progress unfolding.

Once you know how you will be able to tell if you have achieved a specific goal, it is important to keep a visual record of your progress that you can look back on in times of hardship to snap your mind out of trying to make excuses. The visual proof of effort already exerted can be a powerful motivator when it comes to silencing excuses and making goals seem more attainable which in turn keeps motivation high throughout the ordeal. This is especially true once you have reached the halfway point as everything after that is downhill when compared with the effort you have already put in.

Keeping detailed notes of your progress can be as simple as charting your progress on a graph or as complicated as keeping a detailed journal of your experiences. Try various methods of keeping track of your progress and see which works best for you. Having this record will help to keep the entirety of the goal in the appropriate perspective as well as helping to mitigate any concerns and excuses you might have about not making any headway to your ultimate goal.

Attainable: SMART Goals are always attainable. Ideal scenarios are nice, but including goals that have only a slim probability of materializing is doing little more than wasting your time. This is not say that complicated or difficult goals should be avoided, rather it is about realistically knowing your limits and when they can be expanded. Setting long-term goals is good for the self-image of the business and it can help every member of the team grow in an attempt to reach them.

Relevant to your current situation: It is important that the goal you choose is relevant to your current situation as well as being simply something that is attainable with only a reasonable amount of effort. Relevance is key to turning the SMART goal system from a one-time thing into a pattern and eventually a life-long habit that you can rely on to help you meet the challenges of life no matter what they may be. Remember, you want these early goals to be as meaningful as possible so that you think back on them regularly and fortify the neural pathways as quickly as possible so they become your brain's default way of acting.

If you take it slow you will find that completing part of the task related to achieving your current goal will become a habit just like anything else which will thin make it easier to work on even more complicated tasks in turn. As with everything else described above, when working on cementing SMART goals in your life you will want to remember that practice makes perfect.

SMART goals are timely: Studies show that you are statistically more likely to continue to works towards the completion of a complicated or difficult task if it has a deadline associated with it. What this means is that you will want to determine what your ultimate goal will be, determine a timeline for completion, and then do the same for each of the sub-goals you set as well. When it comes to setting a due date for your goals, you will want to consider periods of time that are long enough to allow you to realistically experience a few setbacks along the way, without being so lax that you never actually get around to accomplishing anything. What you are shooting for is something that will force you to stop dreaming about financial freedom and start working towards it, not something so strict that you have no realistic chance of success.

Track your progress

Instead of being in a rush to look into how effective your plan is or setting daily trading goals that are, frankly, completely unrealistic, especially so early on, you will want to make a point of sticking to the plan that you created and keeping detailed notes on every single trade that you make, what the results are and what all of the relevant details turned out to be. To determine the metrics that are most relevant to your overall success, you are going to want to first ask yourself what type of trader you are.

If you are someone who is always hunting for big risks and bigger rewards, then you will be much better served by finding out how successful you have been overall in a given time period (starting with one month of data) as opposed to the number of successful or unsuccessful trades. On the other hand, if your overall number of trades is very low because you only make extremely safe moves, then you will want to ensure that each trade you make is as profitable as possible.

Chart your success: After you have waited long enough that you have some data that can be genuinely useful to you, the next thing you are going to want to do is chart out how effective your initial trading plan has been so far. Charting out this type of data will make it easier for you to see if all of the rules you are basing your trading decisions on hold up to a critical analysis. This will help you to determine if the plan that you are working with is going to be reliable moving forward to help to assure yourself that it is going to continue to line up with the goals you have for profit generation. This is also a way to create the baseline for future historical volatility analysis.

Once you have charted out the data that you have so far, the next thing you are going to want to do is to create a summary that reflects the details in the data that you have generated so far. You will want this summary to include all of the details of every single trade that you made in your first month of trading. Seeing all of this data, clear of any daily biases will make it much easier for you to ultimately see the forest, not the trees.

This broader focus will, in turn, make it easier to determine not just how profitable your venture has been thus far but also to illuminate patterns ultimately related to either failure or success that may be hiding in the apparently random data. The more you study your results, the more likely it is that you will be able to turn apparently random instances of good luck into a repeatable pattern of success.

Results that matter most: If you have been following along as suggested, then by now you will certainly have all the data you could ever need when it comes to determining the efficacy of your system. Luckily, you aren't going to need to use all of it regularly, and can instead rely on a few important indicators that will tell you what you really need to know.

- Net profit: To determine the total net profit that you have brought in by trading options thus far, all you need to do is add up all of the profitable trades that you have made thus far and compare that number to the total number of trades where you lost money and determine which number is higher. This is the most basic and broad determination of whether or not your plan is successful if the number you end up with is negative, it is time to go back to square one and find a more profitable plan, anything else is akin to burning money.

- Profit factor: Once your total net profit is facing the right way, the next thing you are going to need to consider how much you are likely to make on your plan per dollar spent assuming everything else remains equal. To find this number you simply take your total profit number and divide it by the total amount of any losses you had. This number needs to be above 1 in order to indicate a profitable plan and anything higher is extremely profitable.

- Percent profitable: You can think of the percent your plan is profitable as how likely you are to win at any given trade. To determine what the number is you simply take the number of trades that ended in success and divide it by the total number of trades that you attempted. There is no target number in this scenario, as the right number depends on whether you prefer major gains and higher risks, in which case you should aim for few trades with higher margins; or you will want a high number if you prefer lots of small, safe trades.

- Trade average net profit: The trade average net profit is the amount you are likely to make on each trade you complete, given your past history of trading. To find this number all you need to do is divide the total amount of profit you made by the total number of trades, regardless of whether or not they were ultimately successful. This number should be positive, and ideally, the higher the better.

If the number ends up being negative, then you need to stop trading until you come up with a plan that is somewhat more effective. When finding this number it is important to leave out any trades that you may have made that were extreme outliers compared to all of your other trades as they can skew this number to the point of irrelevance.

Chapter 3: Fundamental Analysis

While it should come as no surprise that you are going to need to gather as much data as possible in order to make the best trades, regardless of what market you are working in; it is important to keep in mind that if you don't use it in the right way then it is all for naught. There are two ways to get the most out of any of the data that you gather, the first is via technical analysis and the second is via fundamental analysis. As a general rule, you will likely find it helpful to start off with fundamental analysis before moving on to technical analysis as the need arises.

To understand the difference between the two you may find it helpful to think about technical analysis as analyzing charts while fundamental analysis looks at specific factors based on the underlying asset for the market that you are working in. The core tenant of fundamental analysis is that there are related details out there that can tell the whole story when it comes to the market in question while technical analysis believes that the only details that are required are those that relate to the price at the moment. As such, fundamental analysis is typically considered easier to master as it all relates to concepts less expressly related to understanding market movement exclusively. Meanwhile, technical analysis is typically faster because key fundamental analysis data often is only made publicly available on a strict, and limited, schedule, sometimes only a few times a year meaning the availability for updating specific data is rather limited.

Fundamental Analysis Rules

The best time to use fundamental analysis is when you are looking to gain a broad idea of the state of the market as it stands and how that relates to the state of things in the near future when it comes time to actually trading successfully. Regardless of what market you are considering, the end goals are the same, find the most effective trade for the time period that you are targeting.

Establish a baseline: In order to begin analyzing the fundamentals, the first thing that you will need to do is to create a baseline regarding the company's overall performance. In order to generate the most useful results possible, the first thing that you are going to need to do is to gather data both regarding the company in question as well as the related industry as a whole. When gathering macro data, it is important to keep in mind that no market is going to operate in a vacuum which means the reasons behind specific market movement can be much more far reaching than they first appear. Fundamental analysis works because of the stock market's propensity for patterns which means if you trace a specific market movement back to the source you will have a better idea of what to keep an eye on in the future.

Furthermore, all industries go through several different phases where their penny stocks are going to be worth more or less overall based on general popularity. If the industry is producing many popular penny stocks, then overall volatility will be down while at the same time liquidity will be at an overall high.

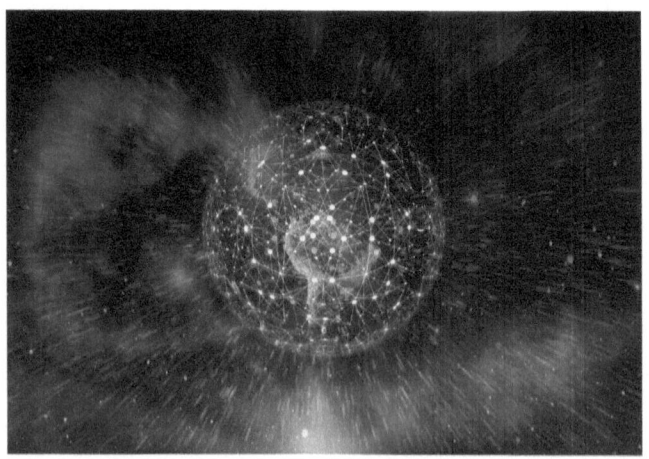

Consider worldwide issues: Once you have a general

grasp on the current phase you are dealing with, the next thing you will want to consider is anything that is going on in the wider world that will after the type of businesses you tend to favor in your penny stocks. Not being prepared for major paradigm shifts, especially in penny stocks where new companies come and go so quickly, means that you can easily miss out on massive profits and should be avoided at all costs.

To ensure you are not blindsided by news you could have seen coming, it is important to look beyond the obvious issues that are consuming the 24-hour news cycle and dig deeper into the comings and goings of the nations that are going to most directly affect your particular subsection of penny stocks. One important worldwide phenomenon that you will want to pay specific attention to is anything in the realm of technology as major paradigm shifts like the adoption of the smartphone, or the current move towards electric cars can create serious paradigm shifts.

Put it all together: Once you have a clear idea of what the market should look like as well as what may be on the horizon, the next step is to put it all together to compare what has been and what might to what the current state of the market is. Not only will this give you a realistic idea of what other investors are going to do if certain events occur the way they have in the past, you will also be able to use these details in order to identify underlying assets that are currently on the cusp of generating the type of movement that you need if you want to utilize them via binary option trades.

The best time to get on board with a new underlying asset is when it is nearing the end of the post-bust period or the end of a post-boom period depending on if you are going to place a call or a put. In these scenarios, you are going to have the greatest access to the freedom of the market and thus have the access to the greatest overall allowable risk that you are going to find in any market. Remember, the amount of risk that you can successfully handle without an increase in the likelihood of failure is going to start decreasing as soon as the boom or bust phase begins in earnest so it is important to get in as quickly as possible if you hope to truly maximize your profits.

Understand the relative strength of any given trade: When an underlying asset is experiencing a boom phase, the strength of its related fundamentals is going to be what determines the way that other investors are going to act when it comes to binary options trading. Keeping this in mind it then stands to reason that the earlier a given underlying asset is in a particular boom phase, the stronger the market surrounding it is going to be. Remember, when it comes to fundamental analysis what an underlying asset looks like at the moment isn't nearly as important as what it is likely to look like in the future and the best way to determine those details is by keeping an eye on the past.

Quantitative Fundamental Analysis

The sheer volume of data and a large amount of varying numbers found in the average company's financial statements can easily be intimidating and bewildering for conscientious investors who are digging into them for the first time. Once you get the hang of them, however, you will quickly find that they are a goldmine of information when it comes to determining how likely a company is to continue producing reliable dividends in the future.

At their most basic, a company's financial statements disclose the information relating to its financial performance over a set period of time. Unlike with qualitative concepts, financial statements provide cold, hard facts about a company that is rarely open for interpretation.

Important statements

Balance sheet: A balance sheet shows a detailed record of all of a company's equity, liabilities and assets for a given period of time. A balance sheet shows a balance to the financial structure of a company by dividing the company's equity by the combination of shareholders and liabilities in order to determine its current assets.

In this case, assets represent the resources that the company is actively in control of at a specific point in time. It can include things like buildings, machinery, inventory, cash and more. It will also show the total value of any financing that has been used to generate those assets. Financing can come from either equity or liabilities. Liabilities include debt that must be paid back eventually while equity, in this case, measures the total amount of money that its owners have put into the business. This can include profits from previous years, which are known collectively as retained earnings.

Income statement: While the balance sheet can be thought of as a snapshot of the fundamental economic aspects of the company, an income statement takes a closer look at the performance of the company exclusively for a given timeframe. There is no limit to the length of time an income statement considers, which means you could see them generated month to month, or even day to day; however, the most common type used by public companies are either annual or quarterly. Income statements provide information on profit, expenses, and revenues that resulted from the business that took place over the specific period of time.

Cash flow statement: The cashflow statement frequently shows all of the cash outflow and inflow for the company over a given period of time. The cash flow statement often focuses on operating cash flow which is the cash that will be generated by day to day business operations. It will also include any cash that is available from investing which is often used as a means of investing in assets along with any cash that might have been generated by long-term asset sales or the sale of a secondary business that the company previously owned. Cash due to financing is another name for money that is paid off or received based on issuing or borrowing funds.

The cash flow statements are quite important as it is often more difficult for businesses to manipulate it when compared to many other types of financial documents. While accountants can manipulate earnings with ease, it is much more difficult to fake having access to cash in the bank where there is none that really exists. This is why many savvy investors consider the cash flow statement the most reliable way to measure a specific company's performance.

Finding the details: While tracking down all the disparate financial statements on the company's you are considering purchasing stock in can be cumbersome, the Securities and Exchange Commission (SEC) requires all publicly traded companies to submit regular filings outlining all of their financial activities including a variety of different financial statements. This also includes information such as managerial discussions, reports from auditors, deep dives into the operations and prospects of upcoming years and more.

These types of details can all be found in the 10-K filing that each company is required to file every year, along with the 10-Q filing that they must send out once per quarter. Both types of documents can be found online, both at the corporate website for the company as well as on the SEC website. As the version that hits the corporate site doesn't need to be complete, it is best to visit SEC.gov and get to know the Electronic Data Gathering, Analysis, and Retrieval system (EDGAR) which automates the process of indexing, validating, collecting, forward and accepting submissions. As this system was designed in the mid-90s, however, it is important to dedicate some time to learning the process as it is more cumbersome than 20 years of user interface advancements have to lead you to expect.

Qualitative Fundamental Analysis

Qualitative factors are generally less tangible and include things like its name recognition, the patents it holds and the quality of its board members. Qualitative factors to consider include:

Business model: The first thing that you are going to want to do when you catch wind of a company that might be worth following up on is to check out its business model which is more or less a generalization of how it makes its money. You can typically find these sorts of details on the company website or in its 10-K filing.

Competitive advantage: It is also important to consider the various competitive advantages that the company you have your eye on might have over its competition. Companies that are going to be successful in the long-term are always going to have an advantage over their competition in one of two ways. They can either have better operational effectiveness or improved strategic positioning. Operational effectiveness is the name given to doing the same things as the competition but in a more efficient and effective way. Strategic positioning occurs when a company gains an edge by doing things that nobody else is doing.

Changes to the company: In order to properly narrow down your search, you will typically find the most reliable results when it comes to companies that have recently seen major changes to their corporate structure as it is these types of changes that are likely to ultimately precede events that are more likely to see the company jump to the next level. The specifics of what happened in this instance are nearly as important as the fact that statistically speaking, 95 percent of companies that experience this type of growth started with a significant change to the status quo.

Chapter 4: Technical Analysis

When working with technical analysis you are always going to want to remember that it functions because of the belief that the way the price of a given trade has moved in the past is going to be an equally reliable metric for determining what it is likely to do again in the future. Regardless of which market you choose to focus on, you'll find that there is always more technical data available than you will ever be able to realistically parse without quite a significant amount of help. Luckily, you won't be sifting through the data all on your own, and you will have numerous technical tools including things such as charts, trends, and indicators to help you push your success rates to new heights.

While some of the methods you will be asked to apply might seem arcane at first, the fact of the matter is that all you are essentially doing is looking to determine future trends along with their relative strengths. This, in turn, is crucial to your long-term success and will make each of your trades more reliable practically every single time.

Understand core assumptions: Technical analysis is all about measuring the relative value of a particular trade or underlying asset by using available tools to find otherwise invisible patterns that, ideally, few other people have currently noticed. When it comes to using technical analysis properly you are going to always need to assume three things are true. First and foremost, the market ultimately discounts everything; second, trends will always be an adequate predictor of price and third, history is bound to repeat itself when given enough time to do so.

Technical analysis believes that the current price of the underlying asset in question is the only metric that matters when it comes to looking into the current state of things outside of the market, specifically because everything else is already automatically factored in when the current price is set as it is. As such, to accurately use this type of analysis all you need to know is the current price of the potential trade in question as well as the greater economic climate as a whole.

Those who practice technical analysis are then able to interpret what the price is suggesting about market sentiment in order to make predictions about where the price of a given cryptocurrency is going to go in the future. This is possible due to the fact that pricing movements aren't random. Instead, they follow trends that appear in both the short and the long-term. Determining these trends in advance is key to using technical analysis successfully because all trends are likely to repeat themselves over time, thus the use of historical charts in order to determine likely trends in the future.

When it comes to technical analysis, the what, is always going to be more important than the why. That is, the fact that the price moved in a specific way is far more important to a technical analyst then why it made that particular movement. Supply and demand should always be consulted, but beyond that, there are likely too many variables to make it worthwhile to consider all of them as opposed to their results.

Price charts

Technical analysis is all about the price chart which is a chart with an x and y axis. The price is measured along the vertical axis and the time is measured via the horizontal axis. There are numerous different types of price charts that different types of traders prefer, these include the point and figure chart, the Renko chart, the Kagi chart, the Heikin-Ashi chart, the bar chart, the candlestick chart, the line chart, and the tick chart. However, the ones you will need to concern yourself with at first are going to be included in any forex trading platform software and are the bar chart, the candlestick chart, the line chart, and the point and click chart which is why they are outlined in greater detail below.

Line chart: Of all the various types of charts, the line charts is the simplest because it only presents price information in the form of closing prices in a fixed time span. The lines that give it its name are created when the various closing price points are then connected with a line. When looking at a line chart it is important to keep in mind that they will not be able to provide an accurate visual representation of the range that individual points reached which means you won't be able to see either opening prices or those that were high or low prior to close. Regardless, the closing point is important to always consider which is why this chart is so commonly referred to by technical traders of all skill levels.

Bar chart: A bar chart takes the information that can be found in a line chart and expands upon it in a number of interesting ways. For starters, the chart is made using a number of vertical lines that provide information on various data points. The top and bottom of the line can then be thought of as the high and low of the trading timeframe respectively while the closing price is also indicated with a dash on the right side of the bar. Furthermore, the point where the currency price opened is indicated via a dash and will show up on the left side of the bar in question.

Candlestick chart: A candlestick chart is similar to a bar chart, though the information it provides is much more detailed overall. Like a bar chart it includes a line to indicate the range for the day, however, when you are looking at a candlestick chart you will notice a wide bar near the vertical line which indicates the degree of the difference the price saw throughout the day. If the price that the stock is trading at increases overall for the day, then the candlestick will often be clear while if the price has decreased then the candlestick is going to be read.

Point and figure chart: While seen less frequently than some of the other types of charts, a point and figure chart has been around for nearly a century and can still be useful in certain situations today. This chart can accurately reflect the way price is going to move, though it won't indicate timing or volume. It can be thought of as a pure indicator of price with the excessive noise surrounding the market muted, ensuring nothing is skewed.

A point and figure chart is noticeable because it is

made up of Xs and Os rather than lines and points. The Xs will indicate points where positive trends occurred while the Os will indicate periods of downward movement. You will also notice numbers and letters listed along the bottom of the chart which corresponds to months as well as dates. This type of chart will also make it clear how much the price is going to have to move in order for an X to become an O or an O to become an X.

Trend or range: When it comes to using technical analysis successfully, you will want to determine early on if you are more interested in trading based on the trends you find or on the range. While they are both properties related to price, these two concepts are very different in practice which means you will want to choose one to emphasize over the other. If you decide to trade according to trend, then you are more interested in going with the flow and choosing stocks to trade while everyone else is having the same idea.

Chart Patterns to Be Aware Of

Flags and Pennants: Both flags and pennants show retracement, that is deviations that will be visible in the short term in relation to the primary trend. Retracement results in no breakout occurring from either the resistance or support levels but this won't matter as the security will also not be following the dominant trend. The lack of breakout means this trend will be relatively short term. The resistance and support lines of the pennant occur within a larger trend and converge so precisely that they practically form a point. A flag is essentially the same except that the resistance and support lines from the flag will be essentially parallel instead.

If you are looking for them, both flags and pennants are more likely to be found in the mid-section of the primary phase of the trend. They can last up to two weeks before being absorbed back into the primary trend line. They are typically associated with falling volume which means that if you notice a flag or a pennant and the volume is not falling then you are more likely actually seeing a reversal which is an actually changing trend instead of a simple retracement.

Head Above Shoulders Formation: If you are looking for indicators of how long any one particular trend is likely to continue, then looking for a grouping of three peaks in a price chart, known as the head above shoulders formation, can indicate a bearish pattern moving forward. The peaks to the left and to the right of the primary peak, also known as the shoulders, should be somewhat smaller than the head peak and also connect at a specific price. This price is known as the neckline and when it reaches the right shoulder the price will likely then plunge noticeably.

The inverse head and shoulders (or head and shoulders bottom) is a sign that the price of the security in question is about to rise in the face of an existing downward trend. It typically forms at the lowest overall price of the trend.

Based on the analysis of the peak-and-trough pattern from the Dow Theory, an upward trend is then seen as indicative of a series of successive rising troughs and peaks. Meanwhile, a downward trend is indicative of a series of lower peaks and deeper troughs. If this is the case, then the head and shoulders pattern represents a weakening of an existing trend as the troughs and peaks deteriorate.

The head and shoulders top forms at the peaks of an upwards trend and signals that a reversal is often forthcoming through a process of four steps. The first of these starts with the creation of the far-left shoulder which can be formed when the cryptocurrency reaches a new high before dropping to a new low. This is then followed by the formation of the head which occurs when the security reaches an even higher high before retracing back to the low found in the left shoulder. Finally, the right shoulder is formed from a high that is lower than the high found in the head, countered by a retracement back to the low of the left shoulder. The pattern is then completed when the price drops back below the neckline.

The inverse head-and-shoulders pattern is the exact opposite of the head-and-shoulders top, as it signals that the security is set to make an upward move. Often coming at the end of a downtrend, the inverse head and shoulders are considered to be a reversal pattern, as the security typically heads higher after the completion of the pattern.

In both instances, the price dipping below the

neckline signals the true reversal of the trend in question which means the security will now be moving in the opposite direction. This breakout point is often the ideal point to go either short or long depending. It is important to keep in mind, however, that the security is unlikely to continue smoothly in the direction the pattern suggests. As such, you will want to keep an eye out for what is called a throwback move.

Gann: While not universally trusted, Gann indicators have been used by traders for decades and remain a useful way of determining the direction a specific currency is likely to move next. Gann angles are used to determine certain elements of the chart include price, time and pattern which makes it easier to determine the future, past and even present of the market as well as how that information will determine the future of the price.

While you could be forgiven for thinking they are similar to trend lines, Gann angles are actually a different beast entirely. They are, in fact, a series of diagonal lines that move at a fixed rate and can likely be generated by your trading program. When they are compared to a trend line you will notice the Gann angle makes it possible for users to determine a true price at a specific point in the future assuming the current trend continues at its current strength.

Due to the fact that all times exist on the same line, the Gann angle can then also be used to predict resistance, support and direction strength as well as the timing on bottoms and tops as well. Gann angles are typically used to determine likely points of support and resistance and it is easy to get started with as it only requires the trade to determine the proper scale for the chart before drawing in the relevant Gann angles from the primary bottoms to the tops.

Essentially, this means that they make it less complicated for the trader to properly frame the market and thus makes it easier for them to predict the way the market is likely to move in the future based on the way it is currently moving in the predetermined framework. Angles that indicate a positive trend determine support and angles that show a downward trend outline resistance. This means that by understanding the accurate angle of a chart, the trader can more easily determine the best time to buy or sell far more simply than what could otherwise be the case. When utilizing Gann angles it is crucial that you keep in mind all the different things that can potentially cause the market to change between specific angles.

Cup and handle formation: The cup and handle formation most commonly appears if given security reaches a peak price before dropping off significantly for a prolonged amount of time. Sooner than later, however, the security will rebound, which is the perfect time to buy. This is an indicator of a trend that is rapidly rising which means you are going to want to take advantage of it as soon as possible before you miss out.

The handle will form on the cup when those who purchased the security at the previous high-water mark and couldn't wait any longer begin to sell which makes new investors interested who then begin to buy as well. This type of formation does not typically form quickly, and indeed, has been known to take a year or more to become visible.

Ideally, you will then be able to take advantage of this

trend as soon as the handle starts to form. If you see the cup and handle forming, you will still want to consider any other day to day patterns that may be interfering with the overall trend as they are going to go a long way when it comes to determining the actual effectiveness of buying in at a specific point.

Trend lines

Trend lines represent the typical direction that a given underlying asset is likely to move in and, thus, can be very beneficial for traders to highlight prior to trading. This is easier said than done, however, due to the high degree of volatility that assets of all types experience on a regular basis. As such, you will find it much more useful to consider only the highs and lows that the underlying asset experiences as this will make it far easier to determine a workable pattern. Once you have determined the highs and the lows for the underlying asset it then becomes much easier to determine if the highs are increasing while the lows are decreasing or vice versa. You will also want to remain alert to the possibility of sidewise trends, where the price doesn't move much of anywhere, as this is a sign that you should avoid trading for the time being.

When watching the trend lines, you will likely notice that the price movement of a given underlying asset tends to bounce off the same high and low points time after time. These are what are known as resistance and support levels and identifying them makes it easier for you to determine the supply and demand of the coin in question. The support level is the level that the price is unlikely to drop below because there are always going to be traders who are willing to buy at that point, driving demand back up. Once the price reaches the point where traders feel the price is unlikely to go any higher, they start to sell, and a level of resistance is created.

Moving averages: The most commonly used confirmation tool is one that is referred to as the moving average convergence divergence or MACD for short. This tool measures the amount of difference that there is between two averages that have been smoothed to minimize ancillary noise.

The difference between the two results is then further smoothed by the process before then being matched against the moving average that it relates to as well. If the resulting smoothed average is still greater than the existing moving average, then you can be sure that the positive trend you were chasing actually exists. Meanwhile, if the smoothed average ends up below the existing moving average than any negative trends will be confirmed instead.

The moving average convergence divergence indicator is a type of oscillating indicator that primarily moves between zero and the centerline. If the MACD value is high then you can assume the related underlying asset is nearly overbought and if the value is low, then the stock is nearly oversold.

The MACD chart is typically based on a combination of several EMAs. These averages can be based on any timeframe, though the most common is the 12-26-9 chart. This chart is typically broken into multiple parts, the first of which is the 26-day and 12-day chart. Mixing up the EMAs will allow you to more accurately gauge the level of momentum that the trend you are tracking is experiencing.

If the 12-day EMA ends up above the 26-day EMA, then you can assume the underlying stock in on an uptrend and the reverse indicates a downtrend. If the 12-day EMA increases more quickly than the 26-day EMA then the uptrend is going to be even more well-pronounced. However, if the 12-day EMA moves closer to the 26-day EMA then you can safely assume that it is starting to slow, and the momentum is waning, which means it is going to take the trend with it.

The MACD uses the EMA by considering the difference between them once they are plotted out. If the 26-day and the 12-day are the same, then the MACD equal out to 0. If the 12-day ends up at a higher point than the 26-day then you can assume the MACD is positive, if not, it will be negative. The greater the difference between the two, the greater the difference between the MAACD line and zero.

From there, you will then want to take into account the 9-day EMA as well. The 9-day EMA is different in that it determines the trend of the AMCD line as opposed to that of the stock price. As such, if the 9-day EMA smooths out the movement of the MACD line the results are going to be far more manageable.

If the result then generates a trend that indicates a negative amount of divergence, then you can be quite certain that the positive trend that is currently taking place is ultimately going to hit a level of resistance that it simply won't be able to overcome.

Chapter 5: Strategies for Beginners

Covered Call Type A: This is an intermediate level strategy and one that is great for getting your feet wet in more advanced options trading. The premise of this strategy is to hold an asset, while writing calls on the same asset in the short term. You will collect the premiums on the contracts that you do write and will know your total level of exposure based on having all of the values for how much you purchased the underlying asset, how much you sold each contract for, and how many contracts you have in circulation.

Let's cover this with a quick example. For the sake of simplicity, I will not be including the cost of broker fees and will be dealing in single contracts, so only writing options for a total number of shares of 100 or fewer.

Covered Call Type B: In the first type of covered call, you purchased the underlying commodity so that you could write a call option and collect the premium. If the exercise price was met, you already owned the commodity and would simply sell the commodity to the buyer of your call. In a covered call type B, you do not purchase the underlying commodity. Instead, you cover yourself by selling calls on an asset and buying calls with the same exercise price, but a higher strike price on the same asset. This strategy is highly situational, and only works when you can find options that work to your favor for this scenario. For example, let's focus on company X again.

Company X is trading at $3.50 a share. One day you buy a call option for $150 with an exercise price of $4.50 and a strike price of $4.00. The expiration date for this contract is on the 15th of the next month. You also sell a call option on company X for $150 with an exercise price of $4.50 and a strike price of $4.10, also with an expiration date for the 15th of the following month. In this case, you are hoping that the exercise price of $4.50 is met. You are holding a call option that nets you $0.50 per share while also having sold a call option that costs you $0.40 per share.

You are collecting the difference of $0.10 per share; this is your profit. Since the price of the option you bought versus the one you sold was exactly the same, you can do this for many multiples of the same contract, providing the strike price is more favorable on the contract that you bought. In our example, you are making $10 for each option ($0.10 * 100 shares per 1 call). If the exercise price is not met, then your total losses/profits are $0. The contract you sold cancels out the contract that you bought.

Of these two types of covered calls, I recommend type A to beginners, as you will need to be very careful when operating under type B. You need to make sure that the contract prices are the same, yet the contracts you purchased have more favorable strike prices. The only way to allow for this is if you very steadily monitor the options index on that particular asset, in this case, company X. You would have to pay close attention and buy and sell those contracts at the exact same time. In this example, we did not include the brokerage fees; an additional calculation that you would have to make. It is an easy additional step for you to calculate but will be variable depending on the brokerage firm you use.

Bull Call Spread/Vertical Spread: The basic idea of this strategy is that an investor believes a commodity is going to move either upward or downward. They have to make a clear cut decision on which direction they believe a commodity will go, and cannot make money from volatility in the opposite direction from which they assumed. We, therefore, have two types of vertical spreads, one for commodities that rise, and one for commodities that fall. A trader will buy calls or puts, while also selling calls or puts depending on the strategy. This strategy is an evolution of the most basic of call strategies from chapter two, where an investor plans on making money from the change of price of a commodity, but in this case also has some up front profit from the contracts that they sell. As with all methods in this book, this is best detailed with examples.

Upward Movement: Suppose that you believe Best Buy stock is going to go up in the future, either the near future or the long term. The stock is currently trading at $50 per share but you do not have enough money to buy a sizeable position in the company, plus if you do it leaves much of your investment money tied up in a single asset. Instead, you decide to buy several calls on Best Buy stock.

They all have roughly the same strike price and exercise price, but vary on the cost per contract and the expiration dates. For our example, you decide to buy three calls. The strike price for each call is $55 and the exercise price for each is $60. The first contract is $100 and expires in one month, the second is $110 and expires in two months, and the third is $120 and expires in three months. Note that if the exercise price is met the day after you buy all of these contracts, you can use all three contracts to immediately buy the stock at the strike price and sell it right away.

You don't have to wait any period of time before using all three contracts, as long as the exercise price is met. Right now your total risk is $330; the total amount spent on all three calls. You stand to make $1500 if the exercise price is met within the first month, $1000 if the exercise price is met within the second month, and $500 if the exercise price is met within the third month. This is because each call has the same strike and exercise price, with each contract offering at least $500 of revenue (100 shares * $5 profit per share) if the exercise price is met.

Your total profits after factoring for the costs of the options are then $1170, $670, and $170. So far what you have is not all that different from what was done in the beginner strategy of using a call option; the only difference is that there are three options to extend the window of profitability if the exercise price is met. With vertical spread we introduce puts to increase the profitability further.

Since you believe that Best Buy stock is due to rise, selling puts on Best Buy stock to increase the profitability from your calls is a good idea. The puts would only be put to use if the stock price of Best Buy falls, therefore based on your assumption about the stock price you will be able to collect the premiums without having to sell any Best Buy stock. You sell three puts, each with the same strike price and exercise price, but with different expiration dates and prices on the contracts. The strike price on each put is $45 with the exercise price on each being $40. The expirations follow the same as the calls from above, that is to say, one month, two months, and three months down the line.

The contract prices are also the same as above $100, $110, and $120. The purpose of these puts is to cancel out the cost of the calls that were made on Best Buy stock. Before, the only way that Best Buy stock was profitable was if the stock moved upwards; anything else was a net loss. Now, you are starting from a neutral position. Unless the stock price moves upwards or downwards in amounts of $10, your total liability is $0. This is a case where the puts are sold for the same price that you purchased the calls. In most real world scenarios, the prices will not be exactly the same, but you can see the utility in that it reduces the starting cost of positioning yourself to profit from the rise of Best Buy stock.

There are two very important notes about this strategy. One, your risk of exposure is quite large if

Best Buy stock falls below $40 per share and the calls expire. You do not own any shares of Best Buy stock and therefore will have to buy them at market value while selling them at $45 per share. Two, if your calls hit their strike price within the first month and you net $1500, you need to save this money until all of the puts you sold expire. You have to hold onto this money in case Best Buy stock swings to meet the strike price of both the calls that you bought and the puts that you sold. This is an unlikely scenario as the value of Best Buy's stock would have to swing $20, but it needs to be taken into account.

Downward Movement: Making profit from the downward movement of a stock through vertical spreads is altogether a very different strategy. It comes in two types; the first being relatively simple and the second requiring significantly greater capitalization and the use of short selling, a type of put option that is much harder to finalize than a standard option contract. A quick note about short selling; short selling, often just referred to as shorting a stock, is when you are betting that the price of a commodity will fall.

These are contracts that take longer to finalize because they are altogether more complicated than a simple put. An investor needs to make sure that they have the right capitalization should the stock not fall, often a line of credit is involved, and the brokers that work in short selling are far more expensive. For your purposes, avoid short selling for now. It is not that it is beyond a simple strategy, but you will need to have such large capitalization and a level of intimacy with markets that beginners to options trading should not attempt it until they have a few years of trading under their belts. Instead, simply focus on the simple version of a vertical spread through simple calls.

Making money from the downward movement of a stock in the vertical spread relies on selling calls in the time frame in which you think a stock price will fall. A good example of this type of strategy is estimating that a company's stock will fall or not rise because of recent news. Take Apple for instance; suppose that they came out with a product that was universally panned, even before it went on sale. You could assume that the stock price is unlikely to rise, at least in the following financial quarter (three months).
You would sell calls on Apple stock with expiration dates for one month, two months, or three months. Your profit is made by collecting the premiums on the

calls, and your risk comes from the possibility of the exercise price being met should Apple's stock price rise. This strategy is extremely simple and does not require a detailed example. There are a couple of things to note about this method however: one, your potential risk is unlimited. The stock could climb infinitely high before the expiration date on the calls you sell, making this a risky proposition unless you are fairly confident a company's stock price will not increase. Two, you control your level of risk by determining the exercise price. If the exercise price is met then you are forced to sell the stock for the strike price of the call, however, the difference between the trading value of the stock and the exercise price is entirely up to you. It greatly modifies how much the options can be sold for, but also allows the investor to set their level of acceptable risk.

Straddle: The first of our advanced strategies requires the use of both calls and puts to get you into a position of profitability regardless of whether the stock price shifts up or down. This is a great strategy to use in volatile markets where you a wholly unsure of what direction a stock price might shift, but you do believe that it will move up or down. This strategy uses both calls and puts as an insurance mechanism for the movement in either direction. It rests upon buying both calls and puts with the same expiration date and strike price. A major benefit to entering this position is that you know exactly how much risk there is to enter. It is merely a function of the purchase cost of the calls and puts taken on a single commodity.

Suppose that you are interested in taking a straddle position on company Y. Company Y's stock is currently trading at $25 but has moved several times in the last few weeks, with fluctuations of $10 or more. You buy a call and a put on company Y, both with an expiration date of one month from now, a strike price of $25, and exercise prices of $30 and $20 respectively. Each option costs you $250, meaning that it takes $500 to get to this position. Your potential profits here are unlimited if the stock price rises significantly, with still a large amount of profit to be made if the stock price drops far below $20. The $30 and $20 price points are your break even points, but in essence, there are four basic ways in which this straddle can go.

- Case 1: The stock price goes above $30, so you

invoke the call option to buy the stock at $25 a share and sell it at any amount above $30. For example, if the stock price hits $31, your total profit is $100. This is because you sell 100 shares of the stock for $31 while having purchased it at $25, netting you $600. You deduct the cost of getting into this position in the first place to get your total profit of $100. Moving in the upward direction, there is room for unlimited profit. There is no limit to how high the stock price for company Y can go.

- Case 2: The stock price for company Y drops below $20. Let's suppose that it hits $12. This nets you a total profit of $800. You buy the stock for $12 and invoke your put option to sell it at $25. This nets you $1300, minus the $500 to start this position and you get your $800 of profit. The most money you can make from downward movement of the stock price is about $2000; this is if the stock price hits close to $0.
- Case 3: This would be a great scenario, but is altogether very rare. The stock price goes above $30, and before the options expire also

goes below $20. Your profit here is a function of the net revenue made from both options, minus your $500 to buy both options. For example, the stock hits $31, giving you revenue of $600. The stock also hits a low of $18, netting you $700. After deducting the $500 for the options, you take home $800. Again, this is extremely rare, but with a highly volatile stock could happen.

- Case 4: The stock does not move above $30, and also does not drop below $20. In this case, you have lost your total buy in cost of $500. This sum is the total risk that you exposed yourself to so that you could enter this position.

Strangle: A strangle strategy is very similar to the straddle with one minor difference. One of the options is more favorable than the other and is likely to cost a different amount to enter the position. A trader makes money through the volatility of the stock price hoping that it goes above or below the exercise price of the call or put, respectively. Let's take a look at a strangle using an example.

Suppose that you are interested in Dunkin Donut's stock for a strangle position. You believe that there is a period of volatility because coffee bean prices are set to either increase or decrease dramatically. The stock is currently trading at $55. You purchase a call option with a strike price of $58 and an exercise price of $60 for $100. You also purchase a put option with a strike price of $53 and an exercise price of $45 for $70. Notice that the call option is considerably more expensive than the put option.

This is because the call option has a much more favorable exercise price than the put option. You would make this type of trade if you believed that Dunkin's stock is going to fluctuate and that in all likelihood it will go down. At the same time, you believe there is a chance that it could rise, but that it would do so very marginally. Your total cost for getting into this position is $170; the cost of the two options. If Dunkin's stock goes above $58, then the call option can be used to buy the stock at $55 and then be sold at a value above $58. Same for the put option, with the difference being the stock can be bought at $45 and sold at $53.

Determining the true profitability of a strangle is far more complicated than doing the same for a straddle. For example, if Dunkin's stock ended at $63, the profit is calculated with the net revenue of $500 ($63-$58 * 100 shares) minus the buy in cost of both options $170, with a net profit of $330. If the stock price of Dunkin drops to $40, the revenue is $1300 ($53-$40 * 100 shares). The profit is $1130 since you deduct the cost of the two options. The breakeven points are much harder to determine as well, making this an advanced level strategy.

Chapter 6: Options Trading in the Forex Market

The foreign exchange currency market, or forex as it is typically called, is, without a doubt, the most lucrative investment market in the world. Each day it trades more than 4 trillion dollars which is approximately 10 times as much as the New York Stock Exchange. Despite this massive amount of trading, it was difficult for individual traders to take advantage of the market due to the technological limitations of the time. This is no longer the case, however, as the internet has given rise to numerous forex trading platforms which means that now forex trading is open to everyone.

Unlike many other types of markets, the forex market is purely speculative which means that nothing is actually changing hands when you place a forex trade. Rather, the forex market essentially only exists on various servers and databases worldwide with information coming in from countries all over the world causing these numbers to move in one direction or another. Each transaction is then tracked with any potential losses or gains expressed in the primary currency of the country the database that is accessing the information is located in.

While this might seem like an odd system, it makes sense when you realize that the only reason the forex market exists is that major corporations and countries needed a way to convert currencies from one type to the other without going through a lot of cumbersome steps to do so. These major players tend to move amounts of currency that are vast enough to affect the actual value of the currencies being traded which is where the speculative portion of the equation comes into play.

Currently, only about 20 percent of the activity related to the forex market comes from these major players with the rest instead of coming from investors who are looking to make money based on the way the various currencies are reacting to the current market. A majority of these traders are professionals who work for financial institutions or hedge funds though more and more freelance traders are jumping on the forex bandwagon every day.

Forex basics: The most important thing to keep in mind when it comes to forex trading is that forex trades always consist of a pair of currency rather than a single asset like you would see in the stock or options market. What this means is that for every trade a forex trader is buying one currency and selling another. Currency is typically traded in 3 differing quantities, known as lots. A micro lot is 1,000 currency units, a mini lot is 10,000 units and a standard lot is 100,000 units.

The smallest amount that a given currency can move is one percent of its current total which is referred to as a pip. When you are first starting out with forex trading then it is recommended that you trade in micro lots as a single pip there is only work 10 cents of the currency in question. This means you will have less at stake during the early days when you are still finding your footing and you may often find yourself fighting against a market that has turned against you in unexpected ways. If you instead start with mini lots then with each pip of movement you are risking $10. To put this into perspective, the market frequently moves 100 pips or more in an average trading session.

While the forex market has several unique features that set it apart from other equities markets, it is the same in the ways that matter the most. Specifically, it is still driven by the core concept of supply and demand. As such, if a certain currency is experiencing high demand, then the value of that currency will increase accordingly until it reaches a point of oversaturation whereupon it will start to move back in the other direction. This means that as a forex trader you are going to need to be aware of when a given currency is going to increase in demand so that you can buy into it at the lowest price possible and thus reap the greatest rewards. This means you will always need to be aware of key interest rate movements, economic predications, and geopolitical strife.

Another important fact to keep in mind is that from Monday morning to Friday evening, the forex market never closes. Despite this fact, currency pairs are typically only traded during the times of day when the country whose currency it is are most active. Each trading day is generally broken into 3 chunks, Europe, US and Asia with the related currency pairs being traded during those periods.

This is the case because the currency pairs of those

regions are always going to be more valuable during the periods of prime activity for the region in question. As an example, if you were thinking about trading a pair based around the US dollar and the Japanese yen then you would find that pair to be most profitable during the US hours and again during the Asian hours.

While there are currency pairs for essentially every combination of currency imaginable, the majority of forex trading can be broken down into 18 primary pairs. These 18 pairs are, in turn, made up of just 8 currencies that you are going to need to be familiar with if you hope to find success in the forex market. These are AUD the Australian dollar, CAD the Canadian dollar, CHF the Swiss franc, EUR the euro, GBP the British pound, JPY the Japanese yen, NZD the New Zealand dollar and USD the US dollar. Knowing what currencies to focus on and which to ignore, at least up front, is crucial to making the early days of forex trading as manageable as possible. There will be plenty of time for exploring lesser used currencies later, once you are completely comfortable with the basics.

Short-term strategy: If you are interested in trading

options in the forex market in the short term then it is important to keep in mind that your goal should always be to control the amount of risk you take on as much as possible. This will make it easier for you to deal in charts that tend to offer shorter time frames than many forex traders deal in. This doesn't mean that you are going to want to stick to the short-term charts exclusively, however, as this can cause your profits to be lower overall than they would otherwise be.

To trade effectively in the short-term, the first thing you are going to want to be on the lookout for is a pair of moving averages on the hourly charts. The trading platform that you use should be able to automatically generate what you are looking for based on the timeframe that you choose. After you have the indicators that you are looking for, you will then be able to more easily utilize them as a sort of guidepost that will make it easier to determine how the market is moving in the timeframe in question so that you will be able to look before you leap as it were. If the resulting short moving average is less than the larger moving average then you will want to take a long position, otherwise, you will want to take a short position instead.

Once you have determined the trend that you are looking for, the next thing you will need to do is to look at the entries that are going to match the direction of the trend you are following. The goal here should be to successfully locate the momentum that you saw on the longer chart in either the 15-minute or 5-minute chart that you will actually want to do work in.

When putting this strategy to use, it is crucial that you keep in mind that it will not always be the right time to buy in. Instead, you are going to need to be patient and wait for a position that is profitable to open up and the best way to do so is to look for the exponential moving average. When seeking out the exponential moving average you are going to want to start by finding a trigger known as the 8-period exponential on the 5-minute chart which should be available from your trading platform. When this exponential starts to move in the direction of the trend you are following then you will know that it is a good time to go ahead and buy in.

While this strategy requires a good deal of

micromanaging in order to be successful, it is also beneficial in several ways. The first of which is that if you choose to wait until you see the right trigger then you know that other traders are already creating action around the currency pair in question which means you can be fairly certain that the trade will be profitable. Additionally, this is a great strategy to use for those who have a lower amount of starter capital as it will make it easier to jump in on a given currency pair before the momentum picks up steam and the bullish nature of the pair causes the price to rise to a less tantalizing point.

In addition to making it easy to buy cheap, those who use this strategy when it comes to selling currency pairs they currently own will be able to do so to maximize their profits as they will be able to get out of a given trade before the masses do so, thus ensuring a higher price when they sell. It is important to remember, however, that the price could instead experience a short-term retracement which means you need to be sure of what the signals are telling you before you make a move if you don't want to pay the price for jumping out early.

In order to ensure a level of maximum profit with this

strategy, you are going to need to set your stop losses at such a point that they are just underneath the last high that the currency experienced. If you are investing in short positions then you will want to set your stop losses so they are just above the current low price point instead. This will ensure that you don't lose out if the trend loses momentum before it reaches the price you are hoping for. By doing so you ensure that the short-term strategy remains as versatile as possible.

This strategy is not without risks of its own, however, as the short-term charts are prone to changing dramatically with little or no advanced notice. This means that if you hope to profit when using this strategy, you are going to need to make sure that you have the ability to react quickly to unexpected changes. The best reaction most of the time is going to be waiting for the currency to settle down before setting a new stop loss based on the new landscape that is slightly in the money without getting greedy.

Fibonacci retracement: To use a Fibonacci retracement, the first thing you are going to want to look for is a market that is trending. The general idea here is to go long on a retracement, a temporary reversal of direction in the price of the currency, at a specific level when the market is positively trending and to go short on retracements when the market is trending in the other direction. To find a retracement level you are going to want to find moments when pricing indicators you are looking for reach high, or low, points that are higher, or lower, than the average high, or low, point.

To understand the Fibonacci ratios that are useful in forex, it is important to understand the basics behind the Fibonacci numbers which were discovered by the man whose name they bear; they start off as 0, 1, 2, 3, 5, 7, 13, 21, etc. Essentially, to find the next number in the sequence you simply add the previous 2 numbers in the sequence together. Now, if you measure the ratio of each number to the following number in the sequence you get the Fibonacci ratios that are used in forex. These start off as .236, .382, .5, .618 etc. While the exact reason that Fibonacci ratios apply to the forex market isn't completely clear, it is clear that they resonate throughout the world at large from the smallest instance in individual molecules of DNA to the grandest in the organization of the planets in the sky.

Luckily, when it comes to utilizing the Fibonacci ratio in your trades, you don't need to memorize these numbers as all forex trading platforms will have a tool that will do the calculations for you. This means that all you really need to do is to learn how, when and why to use them in a technical analysis sense. It is important to keep in mind that Fibonacci levels are going to act as resistance as well as support for the price in question. As the price increases, the Fibonacci levels will act as resistance and as the price decreases, they will act as support. Additionally, much like with regular support or resistance they can be broken.

Trades that are based around the Fibonacci retracement on the charts for timeframes less than 10 minutes. Fibonacci retracements can be used to determine reasonable reward/risk levels either by selling a credit spread to the level in question or through buying options that are already in the money that are likely to experience a bounce at these levels. It is generally going to be in your best interest to look for Fibonacci levels that are likely to overlap at multiple timeframes as well as corresponding to the most recent trend experienced by the underlying stock. If you are so inclined, you can also utilize candlestick price patterns as a means of confirming a buy at specific Fibonacci levels.

Alternately, you may find success with oversold or overbought indicators when it comes to range-bound or trendless stocks. You can then sell credit spreads or buy into options that are already in the money and near the current level of resistance and support with tight stops. It is important to keep in mind that a given stock might not move quickly enough to make these levels worthwhile so it is important to do your research ahead of time in order to have a reasonable expectation about the future movement.

Indicators that are used to signal lower than average volatility such as Bollinger bands are especially useful when it comes to place trades that you anticipate big moves from. Breakout indicators time, especially for the shorter charts, is also especially useful.

Using the Fibonacci sequence to perform a retracement gives you the ability to determine how much an asset moved at price initially. It uses multiple horizontal lines to point out resistance or support at either 23.6, 38.2, 50, 61.8 or 100 percent. When used properly they make it easier to identify the spots transactions should be started, what prices to target and what stop losses to set.

This doesn't mean that you should apply the Fibonacci retracements blindly as doing so can lead to failure as easily as it can success. It is important to avoid choosing inconsistent reference points which can easily lead to mistakes as well as misanalysis, for example, mistaking the wick for the body of a candle. Retracements using the Fibonacci sequence should always be applied wick-to-wick which in turn leads to a clearly defined and actionable resistance level.

Likewise, it is important to always keep the big picture in mind and keep an eye on trends that are of the longer variety as well. Failing to keep a broad perspective in mind makes short-term trades more likely to fail as it makes it harder to project the correct momentum and direction any potential opportunities might be moving in. Keeping the larger trends in mind will help you pick more reliable trades while also preventing you from accidentally trading against a specific trend.

Don't forget, Fibonacci retracements are likely to indicate quality trades, but they will never be able to do so in a complete vacuum. It is best to start with a retracement and then apply other tools including stochastic oscillators or MACD. Moving ahead without confirmation will leave you with little except positive thoughts and wishes that the outcome goes the way you want. Remember, there is no one indicator that is strong enough to warrant moving forward on a trade without double checking the validity of the data.

The other limitation of a Fibonacci retracement is that it doesn't work reliably over shorter time frames as there is simply too much interference from standard market volatility which will result in false apparent levels of support as well as resistance. What's more, the addition of whipsaws and spikes can make it difficult to utilize stops effectively which can result in tight and narrow confluences.

Chapter 7: Tips for Success

Know when to go off book: While sticking to your plan, even when your emotions are telling you to ignore it, is the mark of a successful trader, this in no way means that you must blindly follow your plan 100 percent of the time. You will, without a doubt, find yourself in a situation from time to time where your plan is going to be rendered completely useless by something outside of your control. You need to be aware enough of your plan's weaknesses, as well as changing market conditions, to know when following your predetermined course of action is going to lead to failure instead of success. Knowing when the situation really is changing, versus when your emotions are trying to hold sway is something that will come with practice, but even being aware of the disparity is a huge step in the right direction.

Avoid trades that are out of the money: While there are a few strategies out there that make it a point of picking up options that are currently out of the money, you can rest assured that they are most certainly the exception, not the rule. Remember, the options market is not like the traditional stock market which means that even if you are trading options based on underlying stocks buying low and selling high is just not a viable strategy. If a call has dropped out of the money, there is generally less than a 10 percent chance that it will return to acceptable levels before it expires which means that if you purchase these types of options what you are doing is little better than gambling, and you can find ways to gamble with odds in your favor of much higher than 10 percent.

Avoid hanging on too tightly to your starter strategy: The personalized trading strategy that you created in chapter four if you have been following along, is an important step in trading properly, no two ways around it. That doesn't mean that it is the last strategy that you are ever going to need, however, far from it. Your core trading strategy is one that should always be constantly evolving as the circumstances surrounding your trading habits change and evolve as well. What's more, outside of your primary strategy you are going to want to eventually create additional plans that are more specifically tailored to various market states or specific strategies that are only useful in a narrow band of situations. Remember, the more prepared you are prior to starting a day's worth of trading, the greater your overall profit level is likely to be, it is as simple as that.

Utilize the spread: If you are not entirely risk averse, then when it comes to taking advantage of volatile trades the best thing to do is utilize a spread as a way of both safeguarding your existing investments and, at the same time, making a profit. To utilize a long spread you are going to want to generate a call and a put, both with the same underlying asset, expiration details, and share amounts but with two very different strike prices. The call will need to have a higher strike price and will mark the upper limit of your profits and the put will have a lower strike price that will mark the lower limit of your losses. When creating a spread it is important that you purchase both halves at the same time as doing it in fits and spurts can add extraneous variables to the formula that are difficult to adjust for properly.

Never proceed without knowing the mood of the market: While using a personalized trading plan is always the right choice, having one doesn't change the fact that it is extremely important to consider the mood of the market before moving forward with the day's trades. First and foremost, it is important to keep in mind that the collective will of all of the traders who are currently participating in the market is just as much as a force as anything that is more concrete, including market news. In fact, even if companies release good news to various outlets and the news is not quite as good as everyone was anticipating it to be then related prices can still decrease.

To get a good idea of what the current mood of the market is like, you are going to want to know the average daily numbers that are common for your market and be on the lookout for them to start dropping sharply. While a day or two of major fluctuation can be completely normal, anything longer than that is a sure sign that something is up. Additionally, you will always want to be aware of what the major players in your market are up to.

Never get started without a clear plan for entry and exit: While finding your first set of entry/exit points can be difficult without experience to guide you, it is extremely important that you have them locked down prior to starting trading, even if the stakes are relatively low. Unless you are extremely lucky, starting without a clear idea of the playing field is going to do little but lose your money. If you aren't sure about what limits you should set, start with a generalized pair of points and work to fine tune it from there.

More important than setting entry and exit points, however, is using them, even when there is still the appearance of money on the table. One of the biggest hurdles that new options traders need to get over is the idea that you need to wring every last cent out of each and every successful trade. The fact of the matter is that, as long as you have a profitable trading plan, then there will always be more profitable trades in the future which means that instead of worrying about a small extra profit you should be more concerned with protecting the profit that the trade has already netted you. While you may occasionally make some extra profit ignoring this advice, odds are you will lose far more than you gain as profits peak unexpectedly and begin dropping again before you can effectively pull the trigger. If you are still having a hard time with this concept, consider this: options trading is a marathon, not a sprint, slow and steady will always win the race.

Never double down: When they are caught up in the heat of the moment, many new options traders will find themselves in a scenario where the best way to recoup a serious loss is to double down on the underlying stock in question at its newest, significantly lowered, price in an effort to make a profit under the assumption that things are going to turn around and then continue to do so to the point that everything is completely profitable once again. While it can be difficult to let an underlying stock that was once extremely profitable go, doubling down is rarely if ever going to be the correct decision. If you find yourself in a spot where you don't know if the trade you are about to make is actually going to be a good choice, all you need to do is ask yourself if you would make the same one if you were going into the situation blind, the answer should tell you all you need to know.

If you find yourself in a moment where doubling down seems like the right choice, you are going to need to have the strength to talk yourself back down off of that investing ledge and to cut your losses as thoroughly as possible given the current situation. The sooner you cut your losses and move on from the trade that ended poorly, the sooner you can start putting energy and investments into a trade that still has the potential to make you a profit.

Never take anything personally: It is human nature to build stories around, and therefore form relationships with, all manner of inanimate objects including individual stocks or currency pairs. This is why it is perfectly natural to feel a closer connection to particular trades, and possibly even consider throwing out your plan when one of them takes an unexpected dive. Thinking about and acting on are two very different things, however, which is why being aware of these tendencies are so important to avoid them at all costs.

This scenario happens just as frequently with trades moving in positive directions as it does negative, but the results are always going to be the same. Specifically, it can be extremely tempting to hang on to a given trade much longer than you might otherwise decide to simply because it is on a hot streak that shows no sign of stopping. In these instances, the better choice of action is to instead sell off half of your shares and then set a new target based on the updated information to ensure you are in a position to have your cake and eat it too.

Not taking your choice of broker seriously: With so many things to consider, it is easy to understand why many new option traders simply settle on the first broker that they find and go about their business from there. The fact of the matter is, however, that the broker you choose is going to be a huge part of your overall trading experience which means that the importance of choosing the right one should not be discounted if you are hoping for the best experience possible. This means that the first thing that you are going to want to do is to dig past the friendly exterior of their website and get to the meat and potatoes of what it is they truly offer. Remember, creating an eye-catching website is easy, filling it will legitimate information when you have ill intent is much more difficult.

First things first, this means looking into their history of customer service as a way of not only ensuring that they treat their customers in the right way, but also of checking to see that quality of service is where it needs to be as well. Remember, when you make a trade every second count which mean that if you need to contact your broker for help with a trade you need to know that you are going to be speaking with a person who can solve your problem as quickly as possible. The best way to ensure the customer service is up to snuff is to give them a call and see how long it takes for them to get back to you. If you wait more than a single business day, take your business elsewhere as if they are this disinterested in a new client, consider what the service is going to be like when they already have you right where they want you.

With that out the way, the next thing you will need to consider is the fees that the broker is going to charge in exchange for their services. There is very little regulation when it comes to these fees which means it is definitely going to pay to shop around. In addition to fees, it is important to consider any account minimums that are required as well as any fees having to do with withdrawing funds from the account.

Find a Mentor: When you are looking to go from causal trader to someone who trades successfully on the regular, there is only so much you can learn by yourself before you need a truly objective eye to ensure you are proceeding appropriately. This person can either be someone you know in real life, or it can take the form of one or more people online. The point is you need to find another person or two who you can bounce ideas off of and whose experience you can benefit from. Options trading doesn't need to be a solitary activity; take advantage of any community you can find.

Knowledge is the key: Without some type of information which you can use to assess your trades, you are basically playing at the roulette table. Even poker players show up to the table with a game plan. They can adapt to the circumstances and learn to read other players. That way, they can tell the contenders from the pretenders. Options trading is no different. If you are unable to use the information that is out there to your advantage, then what you will end up with is a series of guesses which may or may not play out. Based purely on the law of averages you have a 50/50 chance of making money. That may not seem like bad odds, but a string of poor decisions will leave you in the poor house in no time.

So, it is crucial that you become familiar with the

various analytics and tools out there which you can use to your advantage. Bear in mind that everyone is going to be looking at the same information. However, it is up to you to figure out what can, or might, happen before everyone else does. This implies really learning and studying the numbers so that you can detect patterns and see where trends are headed, or where trends may reverse. The perfect antidote to that is vision and foresight. Practice building scenarios. Try to imagine what could happen is trends continue. Or, what would happen if trends reversed? What needs to happen in order for those trends to continue or reverse?

When you ask yourself such tough questions, your knowledge and understanding begin to expand. Your mind will suddenly be able to process greater amounts of information while you generate your own contingency plans based on the multiple what ifs. That may seem like a great deal of information to handle, but at the end of the day, any time spent in improving your trading acumen is certainly worth the effort.

TONY TOSON

Chapter 8: Mistakes to Avoid

Inexperienced traders are often warned away from purchasing options that are out of the money as being a greater risk than the ultimate reward is likely to be. While it is true that a short expiration time coupled with an out of the money option will frequently look appealing, especially to those with a smaller amount of trading capital to work with, the issue is that all of these types of options are likely to look equally appealing which leaves them with no way to tell the good from the bad. As a more experienced trader, however, you have many more tools at your disposal than the average novice which means that, while risky, cheap options have the potential to generate substantial returns, as long as you keep the following in mind while trading them.

Mishandling early assignment: Early assignment occurs when a holder exercises an option that you are the writer upon much early that you had anticipated, and at terms that are much less favorable than you had initially hoped. If this happens, it can be easy to become flustered and simply sell as requested, taking a loss in the process. Instead, it is important to consider all the possible options, including purchasing another option for the express purpose of selling it, to ensure that you mitigate the extra costs as completely as possible.

Ignoring the statistics behind options trading: One of the biggest mistakes that most newbie options traders make is that they forget the probability is a real thing. When you check a potential stock before purchasing an option, it's important to understand that the history of an option is important when deciding whether or not you should be investing in it, but so are the odds and probability surrounding whether or not a particular event is going to occur.

For example, a common strategy that investors use is to leverage their money by investing in cheap options so that this will help to prevent big losses on a stock that they actually own shares of. Of course, this is a good strategy, but nothing works one-hundred percent of the time. Make sure that if the rules of probability and simple ratios are telling you to stay away from a deal, you listen to the facts that are staring you in the face. Wishful thinking will come to bite you later on.

Being overzealous: Oftentimes when new options traders finally get their initial plan just right, they become overzealous and start committing to larger trades than they can realistically afford to recover from if things go poorly. It is important to take it slow when it comes to building your rate of return and never bet more than you can afford to lose. Regardless of how promising a specific trade might seem, there is not risk/reward level at which it is worth considering a loss that will take you out of the game completely for an extended period of time. Trade reasonably and trade regularly and you will see greater results in the long term guaranteed.

Not being adaptable: The successful options trades know when to follow their plans but they also know that no plan will be the right choice, even if early indicators say otherwise. There is a difference between making a point of sticking to a plan and following it blindly and knowing which is which is one of the more important indicators of the separation between options trading success and abject failure.

This means it is important to be aware of when and where experimentation and new ideas are appropriate and when it is best to toe the line and gather more data in order to make a well-reasoned decision.

This also means having several different plans in your options trading tool box and not just resolutely sticking to the first one that brings you a modicum of success. This is crucial as there are certain plans that will only work in specific situations and knowing which to use when, in real time, will lead to significantly greater returns on a more reliable basis every single time.

Likewise, an adaptive options trader knows that market conditions can change unexpectedly and is prepared to respond accordingly. This means understanding when the time is right to go in a new direction, regardless of the potential risks that doing so might entail. Sometimes a good trader has to make a leap of faith, and a trader who is successful in the long term knows what signs to look for that indicate this type of scenario is occurring in real time. Unfortunately, this type of foresight cannot be taught, and instead must be found with experience.

As long as you keep the appropriate mindset regarding individual trades, any new strategy that is attempted will result in valuable data, if nothing else. It is important to understand that learning not to use a specific course of action a second time is always valuable, no matter the costs. Working to build this into your core trading mindset will lead you to greater success in a wider variety of situations in the long term.

Ignoring the probability: Always remember that the historical data will not apply to the current trends in the market at all times which means you will always want to consider the probability as well as the odds that the market is going to behave the way it typically does. The odds are how likely the market is to behave as expected and the probability is the ratio of the likelihood of a given outcome. Understanding the probability of certain outcomes can make it easy to purchase the proper options to minimize losses related to holdings of specific underlying stocks. When purchasing cheap options, it is important to remember that they are always going to be cheap for a reason as price is determined by strike price of the underlying stock as well as the amount of time remaining for the option to regain its value, choose wisely otherwise you are doing little more than gambling and there are certainly better ways to gamble than via options trading.

Letting the opinions of other influence your trading: While every day trader is going to have opinions regarding the best way to trade this type of stock or when to use that indicator, the best day traders tend to avoid this advice like the plague and instead work out their own. The only thing you really need to focus on in order to make the right types of trades in the right timeframes is math and anything else is only going to get in the way. Keep in mind that you want to analyze and observe economic and political events, not get caught up in them.

Not dealing with short options properly: While, in theory, it might seem like buying back short options at the last moment is the best choice, this practice is sure to hurt your more than help you in the long run. It may be tempting to hold onto profitable options in order to squeeze the maximum return out of each investment but you need to be aware that the potential for a reversal is always lurking in the shadows. Instead, a good rule of thumb is to buy back options that are currently at 80 percent of your ideal return or higher and let the extra take care of itself. While it may hurt to leave some potential profit on the table, it will improve your overall reliability, netting you a profit in the long run.

Not considering exotic options: An exotic option is one that has a basic structure that differs from either European or American options when it comes to the how and when of how the payout will be provided or how the option relates to the underlying asset in question. Additionally, the number of potential underlying assets is going to be much more varied and can include things like what the weather is like or how much rainfall a given area has experienced. Due to the customization options and the complexity of exotic options, they are only traded over-the-counter.

While they are undoubtedly more complex to get involved with, exotic options also offer up several additional advantages when compared to common options including:

- They are a better choice for those with very specific needs when it comes to risk management.

- They offer up a variety of unique risk dimensions when it comes to both management and trading.

- They offer a far larger range of potential investments that can more easily meet a diverse number of portfolio needs.

- They are often cheaper than traditional options.

They also have additional drawbacks, the biggest of which is that they cannot often be priced correctly using standard pricing formulas. This may work as a benefit instead of a drawback, however, depending on if the mispricing falls in the favor of the trader or the writer. It is also important to keep in mind that the amount of risk that is taken on with exotic options is always going to be greater than with other options due to the limited liquidity each type of exotic option is going to have available. While some types are going to have markets that are fairly active, others are only going to have limited interest. Some are even what are known as dual-party transactions which means they have no underlying liquidity and are only traded when two amiable traders can be found.

Not keeping earnings and dividend dates in mind: It is important to keep an eye on any underlying assets that you are currently working with as those who are currently holding calls have the potential to be assigned early dividends, with greater dividends having an increased chance of this occurrence. As owning an option doesn't mean owning the underlying asset, if this happens to you then you won't be able to collect on your hard-earned money. Early assignment is largely a random occurrence which means that if you don't keep your ear to the ground it can be easy to get caught unaware and be unable to exercise the option before you miss the boat.

Along similar lines, you are going to also always want to be aware of when the earning season is going to take place for any of your underlying assets as it is likely going to increase the price of all of the contracts related to the underlying asset in question. Additionally, you will need to be caught up on current events as even the threat of influential news can be enough to cause a significant spike in volatility and premiums as well. In order to minimize the additional costs associated with trading during these periods, you are going to want to utilize a spread. Doing so will minimize the effect that inflation has on your bottom line.

Chasing bottoms and tops: There are certainly some strategies out there that are effective when used near the turning points of existing trends. These are in the minority, however, which means that picking bottoms and tops is, more often than not, a risky proposition. Unfortunately, it is an all too common mistake for traders to invest money into securities that are either too low or too high, gleefully ignoring the 2 percent rule as they do so. This impulse should be avoided like the plague and replaced with a focus on major inbound price moves instead. Sticking to one side of markets that are range-bound will lead to better long-term results at least 90 percent of the time.

Sticking with relative trends: If a trend is already

well-defined in the market then it is entirely possible that it is going to continue long enough for you to make some money off of it but it is far from a guarantee. The market will naturally fluctuate up to 20 percent of its current average with very little warning, before settling back to the current standard. This means that if you recklessly jump onto a specific trend without doing the required homework you will frequently find yourself making a momentum play that is never going to go anywhere.

Before you make a move regarding a specific trend, there are three distinct timeframes you are going to want to consider first. If you are prone to trading in the short-term then you are going to want to keep an eye on the weekly hourly and daily charts. If you prefer holding onto trades for a longer period of time then daily, weekly and monthly charts are typically going to be more useful.

Conclusion

Thanks for making it through to the end of *Options Trading Easiest Guide*, let's hope it was informative and able to provide you with all of the tools you need to achieve your goals, whatever it is that they may be. Just because you've finished this book doesn't mean there is nothing left to learn on the topic, and expanding your horizons is the only way to find the mastery you seek.

Now that you have made it to the end of this book, you hopefully have an understanding of how to get started trading options, as well as a strategy or two, or three, that you are anxious to try for the first time. Before you go ahead and start giving it your all, however, it is important that you have realistic expectations as to the level of success you should expect in the near future.

While it is perfectly true that some people experience serious success right out of the gate, it is an unfortunate fact of life that they are the exception rather than the rule. What this means is that you should expect to experience something of a learning curve, especially when you are first figuring out what works for you. This is perfectly normal, however, and if you persevere you will come out the other side better because of it. Instead of getting your hopes up to an unrealistic degree, you should think of your time spent dealing with options as a marathon rather than a sprint which means that slow and steady will win the race every single time.

The next step is to stop reading already and to get ready to get started taking advantage of the benefits that are unique to the options market. While it may not be exciting, what this means in practical terms is that it is time for you to get down to business and start doing your homework. While you might want to avoid all of that and jump right in, as previously mentioned all this is likely to do is to nip your options trading career in the bud before it even begins. You will need to start by considering which type of underlying asset you are going to want to pursue if stock market options don't sound that appealing to you.

With this out of the way, you will then need to consider the current state of the market in question and how you can craft a plan to take advantage of those specifics. Remember, haste makes waste, and in this case, waste is going to be all of the money you are throwing away by not taking the time to go through to reach the success that is otherwise almost in reach. Take things slow and you are far more likely to find the success you seek.

Finally, if you found this book useful in anyway, a review on Amazon is always appreciated!

www.ingramcontent.com/pod-product-compliance
Lightning Source LLC
Chambersburg PA
CBHW030014190526
45157CB00016B/2701